"A touching story of artistic ~~~~~~ ~~~~~~

—BRENDAN LEMON, FINANCIAL TIMES

"*The Painted Rocks at Revolver Creek* represents a return to politics, specifically a reckoning with lingering inequalities and the rule of law in modern South Africa. The result is as insightful as Fugard's earlier works, with an embedded layer of nuance that can only come from a seasoned dramatist like Fugard."

—ZACHARY STEWART, THEATERMANIA

"Featuring many of the themes familiar from his past plays, *The Painted Rocks at Revolver Creek* is an intimate theatrical gem . . . This deeply affecting play represents another highlight in Fugard's distinguished career."

—FRANK SCHECK, HOLLYWOOD REPORTER

"A modest, almost oblique, but ultimately explosive look at the new South Africa . . . With this drama, Fugard both describes and once again demonstrates the tangible power of art."

—JONATHAN MANDELL, DC THEATRE SCENE

"Thoughtful and poignant . . . A carefully built play, Fugard broadens the meaning of Nukain's masterpiece by placing that powerful symbol of a man's human dignity in a modern-day context."

—MARILYN STASIO, VARIETY

"Athol Fugard is an institution, literary, theatrical, spiritual and political . . . *The Painted Rocks* is raised up by the rigorous eloquence and compassion of Fugard's writing and the uncompromising clarity of his vision."

—SYLVIE DRAKE, CULTURAL WEEKLY

THE PAINTED ROCKS AT REVOLVER CREEK

BOOKS BY ATHOL FUGARD AVAILABLE FROM TCG

THE PAINTED ROCKS AT REVOLVER CREEK

ATHOL FUGARD

THEATRE COMMUNICATIONS GROUP
NEW YORK
2018

The publication of *The Painted Rocks at Revolver Creek* by Athol Fugard, through TCG's Book Program, is made possible in part by the New York State Council on the Arts with the support of Governor Andrew Cuomo and the New York State Legislature.

TCG books are exclusively distributed to the book trade by Consortium Book Sales and Distribution.

Library of Congress Control Numbers:
2017000959 (print) / 2017006057 (ebook)
ISBN 978-1-55936-522-2 (softcover) / ISBN 978-1-55936-848-3 (ebook)
A catalog record for this book is available from the Library of Congress.

Book design and composition by Lisa Govan
Photos (Front): Leon Addison Brown as Nukain Mabuza, Signature Theatre production, 2015. Photo by Joan Marcus. (Back): Nukain Mabuza sitting on "The Throne," 1975. Photo by René Lion-Cachet; courtesy of the Clarke Mabuza Archive, earthart@africa.com

First Edition, October 2018

For Nukain for inspiration. For Paula for provocation.

ACKNOWLEDGMENTS

Special thanks to my wife Paula Fourie for her input during
the writing process and for supporting me during the staging
of the world premiere of *The Painted Rocks at Revolver Creek*.
I would also like to acknowledge the work of Dr. Dirk Hermann
and Chris van Zyl, who compiled the book *Land of Sorrow:
20 Years of Farm Attacks in South Africa*. The bulk of my
writing took place under the umbrella of the Stellenbosch
Institute for Advanced Study (STIAS), whose generous
support proved invaluable.

The Painted Rocks at Revolver Creek was suggested by the life and work of Nukain Mabuza and the Rock Garden he created in the Mpumalanga Province of South Africa from the mid-1960s to 1980. This play is a work of fiction and is not intended to reflect actual circumstances, events, and persons in his life.

Contents

THE PAINTED ROCKS AT REVOLVER CREEK

The Painted Rocks at Revolver Creek had its world premiere at Signature Theatre (James Houghton, Founding Artistic Director; Erika Mallin; Executive Director) in New York City on April 21, 2015. It was directed by Athol Fugard. The scenic design was by Christopher H. Barreca, the costume design was by Susan Hilferty, the lighting design was by Stephen Strawbridge, the sound design was by Stowe Nelson; the production stage manager was Linda Marvel. The cast was:

NUKAIN MABUZA	Leon Addison Brown
BOKKIE	Caleb McLaughlin
ELMARIE KLEYNHANS	Bianca Amato
JONATHAN SEJAKE	Sahr Ngaujah

The Painted Rocks at Revolver Creek had its West Coast premiere at the Fountain Theatre (Deborah Lawlor, Producing Artistic Director; Stephen Sachs, Co-Artistic Director; Simon Levy, Producing Director) in Los Angeles, California, on October 30, 2015. It was directed by Simon Levy. The scenic design was by Jeffrey McLaughlin, the costume design was by Naila Aladdin-Sanders, the lighting design was by Jennifer Edwards, the sound design and original music were by Peter Bayne; the production stage manager was Rita Cofield. The cast was:

NUKAIN MABUZA	Thomas Silcott
BOKKIE	Philip Solomon
ELMARIE KLEYNHANS	Suanne Spoke
JONATHAN SEJAKE	Gilbert Glenn Brown

The Painted Rocks at Revolver Creek was produced at The Fugard Theatre (Eric Abraham, Founding and Executive Producer; Daniel Galloway, Executive Director) in Cape Town, South Africa, on August 23, 2016. It was directed by Athol Fugard and co-directed by Paula Fourie. The scenic design was by Saul Radomsky, the costume design was by Birrie le Roux, the lighting design was by Mannie Manim, the sound design was by Charl-Johan Lingenfelder; the stage manager was Shawn Crow. The cast was:

NUKAIN MABUZA	Tshamano Sebe
BOKKIE	Likho Mango, Siya Jantjie
ELMARIE KLEYNHANS	Anna-Mart van der Merwe
JONATHAN SEJAKE	Sne Dladla

CHARACTERS

NUKAIN MABUZA: "Tata" to Bokkie, "Outa" to Elmarie. An old black man, a natural innocent who has never lost a childlike capacity for looking at the world with wonder. When we first see him, however, he is a troubled man. He wears a farm laborer's pair of faded denim overalls a size too small, his scrawny ankles visible above a pair of painted tekkies. There is an equally old knitted cap on his head.

BOKKIE: A bright and intelligent young black boy about eleven years old. He is barefoot and wears a faded T-shirt and short khaki trousers. He appears pulling a gaudily painted little wagon, loaded with an assortment of paints—white, black, green, yellow, blue, and red—and brushes together with a plastic bottle of water and a jar filled with turpentine.

ELMARIE KLEYNHANS: A farmer's wife living and working on the family farm, Vredewater. She is an Afrikaner and a devout Christian. When we first see her in Act One, she is in her forties. Having returned from church, she is still wearing the special outfit she reserves for church services. In Act Two, she is twenty years older and appears wearing the clothes necessary for a working day on the farm.

JONATHAN SEJAKE: The young Bokkie of Act One, now a grown man who goes by his real name, Jonathan Sejake. A young, well-educated man in his mid-thirties, full of energy and conviction. He is dressed neatly and is burdened with a heavy backpack.

ACT ONE

———

The summit of a small koppie in the Mpumalanga Province of South Africa in the year 1981. It is crowned by a large rock covered with streaks of guano. It is obviously the favorite resting place of a large bird. Lying around it are smaller rocks covered with brightly colored patterns, which suggest that whoever painted them had a very specific vision.

At the start of the play, we hear the flapping of large wings and the harsh cry of a big bird. This is followed by the agitated voices of Bokkie and Nukain calling out urgently. Bokkie appears first, pulling a wagon.

BOKKIE *(Waving his arms to scare away the bird)*: Hurry, Tata! He's back! He's been shitting on the rock again!

NUKAIN *(From off)*: I'm coming! I'm coming! Chase him, Bokkie!

BOKKIE *(Scrambling onto the rocks and waving his arms at the sky)*: Voetsek! Voetsek!

(An out-of-breath and exhausted Nukain appears.)

NUKAIN: Tell him, Bokkie! Tell him to go! Suka wena! *(Taking off his cap and waving it at the sky)* He must go find his own koppie. Voetsek!

BOKKIE: Go find your own koppie!

NUKAIN: Hamba! Hamba!

(Both of them fall silent as they watch the bird circling overhead.)

I think he hears us.

BOKKIE *(His voice charged with admiration)*: Just look at him, Tata. So high! So very high. *(Holding out his arms like wings)* I wonder what it feels like, Tata . . .

NUKAIN: I don't know what he feels like. He doesn't know what I feel like. All I know is he leaves chicken shit on the Big One.

BOKKIE: He's not a chicken, Tata. He's a crow—a black-and-white crow—the Dominee Crow.

NUKAIN: Call him what you like, Bokkie. All Tata knows is that looks like chicken shit. *(Sitting down wearily on a rock)* This koppie is getting too hard for me to climb.

BOKKIE *(Gesturing to the large summit boulder)*: Must I clean this now, Tata?

NUKAIN: Ja. Make it like it was before the bird shit on it.

(Holding out his arms like wings, Bokkie "flies" down to the wagon. He takes a scrubbing brush and a plastic bottle of water from the wagon and starts to clean the boulder. From time to time, he stops to look up at the sky and the bird circling overhead.)

BOKKIE: Maybe it's like the airplane, Tata. The people inside look down and see everything, just like the crow. One day I will also ride in an airplane and look down. There are pictures like that in the geography book at school. Everything is small. That is what he sees. Not you, Tata, not me, not the dassies on the rocks, just the koppies. And the river. The road looks like a long snake. And the houses, they look like small matchboxes.

(A church bell tolls in the distance. Bokkie looks down.)

Like the church is now. Small.

(Measuring the size of the church with his thumb and fore-finger.)

Just so small. *(He goes on talking as he cleans the rock face)* Do you want to fly in an airplane, Tata?

NUKAIN *(Emphatically)*: Aikona!

BOKKIE: Why not, Tata? It will be nice!

NUKAIN: One day that thing falls out of the sky.

BOKKIE: It can't, Tata.

NUKAIN: Why?

BOKKIE: Because it is an airplane. Airplanes don't fall out of the sky. They got a propeller, Tata.

NUKAIN: The day I see him use his wings like that bird, then I believe you.

BOKKIE *(Looking down at the village, he sees people leaving the church)*: Church is over. They finished singing now. There goes Baas Hennie and the Miesies in the bakkie. *(His attention back to the old man)* The Big One is ready for you now, Tata.

(Nukain is staring at the summit rock.)

Tata . . . The Big One is waiting, Tata.

(Gesturing at the wagon and its contents.)

Blue . . . green . . . yellow . . . white . . . and also the brushes. I washed them all. They are nice and clean. What color do you want first, Tata?

(No response from the old man, who is still staring at the rock.)

Tata! What color?

(Still nothing from the old man.)

Come now, Tata, you must paint.

(Still no reaction from the old man. Bokkie is now frustrated and impatient.)

Two Sundays now we come here with everything, but you do nothing, Tata, just sit and stare at the Big One. *(Offering the old man a brush)* Here is your kwas, Tata. Take it! What color first? Red? Blue? Green?

(Nukain takes the brush, but after staring at it for a few seconds shakes his head.)

What is the matter?
NUKAIN: I take it . . . but I am asking . . . what is this thing?
BOKKIE: Tata? It is a kwas. Your favorite kwas. The one we always use for the flowers.
NUKAIN: I know him, Bokkie. But inside I am thinking . . . why is he so heavy today? But I know why. *(Pointing at*

the summit rock) The Big One is waiting. It is now his time and that is why the kwas is heavy.

BOKKIE: But it's never been heavy before. Look, Tata, look at all your flowers. Remember when you asked me how many it is? I counted them. I went down to the road and I started counting. One, two, three, four, five, six, seven, eight, nine, ten. Every time I counted ten, I picked up a small klippie and I started again. When I counted the last one I came to you, Tata, and I held all the klippies in my hands. Ten times ten is a hundred and then five. One hundred and five!

NUKAIN: Yo! That is many.

BOKKIE: You've painted two more since then, Tata. So today when you paint the Big One it will be . . . one hundred and eight.

NUKAIN: It is just so. Haai, Bokkie . . . that young Tata was full of flowers then. And the kwas also knows it. He knows me. When I give him paint he knows what he must do. Ja! This kwas is *slim*. Me and him make all the flowers together.

BOKKIE: So now you must make a big flower for the Big One, Tata . . . the biggest flower.

(Nukain shakes his head.)

Why not?

NUKAIN: Because I am growing tired all the time . . . and . . .

BOKKIE: And what?

NUKAIN: . . . frightened.

BOKKIE: Frightened? Of what?

NUKAIN *(Pointing at the summit rock)*: Him.

BOKKIE: You are frightened of the Big One?

NUKAIN: Ewe.

BOKKIE: Is it because he is big? Tata, you are just as big as him.

NUKAIN: Aikona! He is bigger than me. And I know that he is my last one . . . so I am frightened.

BOKKIE: But he is only a rock.

NUKAIN: I have got no more flowers in me, Bokkie. So what must I do for him? Must I shit on him like the big bird?

BOKKIE *(Laughing at the scene he imagines)*: Shit on him like the crow . . . how are you going to do that, Tata? Pull off your pants and sit on top of the Big One?

NUKAIN *(Getting up and crossing to where Bokkie is sitting near the wagon)*: Ja . . . laugh at me. This old man is frightened of a rock! I also laugh, because this time it is not the polisie who can make me bangbroek, or Baas Hennie if I make him cross and he tells me that he doesn't want me anymore . . . but a rock. I am frightened of a rock. You see, Bokkie, when I make my first flower . . . *(Pointing)* . . . down there . . . next to the road. After that first one I stood up and I saw him there at the top of the koppie and I looked at him and I shouted out: "Your time will come, Big One!" . . . And I was happy. So all the time the kwas and me make flowers. Every Sunday I come here and make some more flowers, and all the time he is there waiting, and when I look up I laugh at him and call to him again: "I'm coming. Wait for me!" And now . . . here we are. Me and him . . . but I am empty. I got no more flowers in me. So what must I do? *(Beckoning for the bottle of water)* Amanzi.

(Bokkie hands the water bottle to the old man and watches him drink. An idea suddenly occurs to him.)

BOKKIE: Tata, are you hungry? Must I fetch some bread? I will ask the Miesies at the big house.

(Nukain shakes his head.)

Ag, please! I will tell Evelina to put some jam on it . . . appelkooskonfyt. If you eat something, Tata, you will feel better, and not frightened of the Big One anymore. And you will paint him.

NUKAIN: I am not hungry, Bokkie.

(Nukain runs his flattened hand over the surface of the rock. With some difficulty, he then manages to sit down. Resting his back against the big rock, he looks at the landscape spread out before him.)

Somewhere out there is where I started walking, Bokkie. A long time ago. That time I was a young man living with my mama. We were waiting for my papa to come home from his job digging gold for the white man. We waited a long time for him but he never came. What did come was a dry time.

BOKKIE: Dry time, Tata?

NUKAIN *(Shaking his head as he remembers the drought and what it led to, reliving it)*: Haai, Bokkie . . . The mielies die . . . the pumpkins die . . . the cows die . . . and still the rain doesn't come. But then one day Mama also starts to cry because we got no more money to buy food. So I say to myself: "No! I must find work." . . . And so I walk my first road. I walk a long time, Bokkie, and then I find work. Somewhere an old miesies is in her garden and she asks me to carry water to her flowers, and when she sees I work hard she says I must come back tomorrow. So I feed the chickens for her, chop wood, clean windows . . . and I put my pennies in a tin, and every night I shake it and feel good because I see the food I am going to buy for my mama. But then I meet another man from our village and he tells me my mama is gone . . . she got sick and she died. Yo! So many roads.

(Bokkie joins Nukain at the foot of the summit rock and sits beside him.)

From here to there, from there to somewhere else . . . this way, that way . . . Sometimes the sun is hot, sometimes the rain is cold. Sometimes I got pennies in my pocket, many times there is nothing in my pocket. I can't even remember all the roads now, Bokkie, that I walked looking for work.

(He looks down at Bokkie, who is listening to his story intently.)

Maybe one day you will also walk many roads. So let me tell you what you must do. Tie your shoes together and hang them around your neck. Let your feet get old, not your shoes. And then you must sing.

BOKKIE: Sing?

NUKAIN: Yes, sing.

(He softly sings a few bars of "We Majola," a traditional Zulu work song with a strong rhythm.)

You don't know it, do you?

BOKKIE: No, Tata.

NUKAIN: I will teach you.

(He sings a few more bars of the song. Bokkie eventually tries to join in. The little lesson ends with Nukain laughing.)

Walk or work, you must sing. It will help you.

BOKKIE: But isn't it nice to see all the different places? I want to see Johannesburg. My teacher says it is a big, big city, Tata.

NUKAIN: That is not a good place, Bokkie. It eats up our people. Just walk your own roads, and maybe you will also have a Big One watching you, waiting for you.

BOKKIE: What do you mean, Tata?

NUKAIN: I think the Big One here was watching me all the time, waiting for me.

BOKKIE: No, Tata. Our Big One is blind.

(Bokkie's words pull the old man out of his reverie.)

NUKAIN: What you say, Bokkie?

BOKKIE: He hasn't got eyes. He hasn't got ears. He doesn't hear you or see you laughing at him. He is just a big rock.

(A suddenly thoughtful Nukain gets up and walks down from the big rock, then turns around and looks at it. Bokkie waits. Eventually:)

What now? *(No response)* Tata! What are we going to do?

NUKAIN *(Starts to laugh, wagging a finger at the rock)*: Wena . . . your time has come, Big One!

(Without being conscious of it, he starts humming the traditional work song "We Majola" again. Its effect is immediately obvious as we see a slow infusion of energy into the tired old body. Bokkie, watching the transformation in the old man's mood, cannot contain his excitement. He dances around, trying to sing and dance with Nukain.)

Vuka, Nukain! Vuka! Bokkie, get the paint and the kwas.

(An excited Bokkie scrambles to get the old man a tin of paint and a brush. He offers Nukain a brush.)

No, Bokkie. You must take the kwas. You must paint.

BOKKIE: No, Tata.

NUKAIN: Yes. Do it, Bokkie. We are going to give the Big One eyes so that he can see me now when I stand here. Go on, Bokkie. Give him eyes.

BOKKIE: But, Tata . . .

NUKAIN *(Fiercely)*: Do it, Bokkie! Give him eyes. Black eyes, Bokkie. Like I do it on the small rocks.

(After a moment's hesitation, Bokkie starts singing again and paints large black squares.)

BOKKIE: Like that, Tata?

(Nukain fills in the black eyes with white paint. He outlines the eyes with yellow.)

NUKAIN: That is good. Now he can see me. Now he must know it is me. *(Confronting the rock)* Look now, Big One. You see me? Make me there, Bokkie. Make me red because now Tata is feeling full of blood.

(In between the "eyes" on the rock face, Bokkie draws a big red circle to represent a head.)

Give me arms and legs. Make me strong, Bokkie, like I was when I walked the roads.

(Adding a body, arms, and legs, Bokkie completes a stick figure.)

White hair, Bokkie. *(He paints white hair on the figure)* Is good. Now bring the kwas and black paint.

(Bokkie obeys. Nukain holds out the palm of his right hand.)

Now paint my hand black. Go on. Do it, Bokkie.
BOKKIE: But, Tata . . .
NUKAIN: Do it, Bokkie!

(Bokkie obeys. Nukain again reliving his past:)

All those years ago when I get my dompas, the polisie take my duim to make my mark. And I say . . . "Yo! What is this now?" And the polisie say to me: "Listen kaffer, this is your mark. If you are skelm this will help us catch you." *(To the rock)* But you, Big One, I give you my whole hand so that you can catch me with your eyes.

(He goes to the rock and presses his palm on its surface, leaving an impression of his hand.)

Now you know me. Yes, now you see me. And here, Big One, is my fokken dompas that I must have in my pocket all the time, that tells me where I can walk, where I can work. *(To his passbook)* I say voetsek to you as well! You got my mark, not my life.

(Spitting on his passbook, he throws it at the foot of the rock. To the rock once more:)

But what do you see standing here? Old man? Just another old kaffer? No, Big One, I am not old man. I am not kaffer. I am MAN. My hair is white, my skin is black, but I am Man!

(Rolling up his sleeves and defiantly holding up his clenched fists.)

These hands hold the spade, Big One. These hands dig. I fix fences for the boers . . . I plant groente for them . . . tomatoes, potatoes, carrots . . . in the gardens I plant flowers for the Miesies.

(Turning to look out over the land and pointing as he speaks) There . . . and there . . . and there . . . I dig . . . I sweat. Many times I meet brothers and sisters on the road looking for work like me. If I got bread or they got bread we break it and eat and talk. One time it is Amos, another time it is Bongi . . . or Nomhle. They all ask me, "Where is your home?" *(Speaking to the rock)* Can you show me, Big One? My papa and my mama are sleeping in the ground, far away . . . but where is my home? I was born on this land. I walk and work on this land. One day I will die on this land, but I got no home.

(He makes a sweeping gesture to the landscape they can see from the top of the hill) Now look there, Big One! Look out there. You see the land? You see the roads? Do you see me walking the roads?

(Taking a brush and the tin of black paint) The black roads I walk . . .

(Painting thick, spaced vertical lines underneath the stick figure as he talks.)

This way, now that way . . . From Doornberg to Bitterfontein, Bitterfontein to Rietvlei, from Rietvlei to Excelsior, then Kanonkop . . . Kanonkop to Jagtersnek.

(Now filling in the spaces between the black lines with white paint.)

I walk a long time . . . From me to him.

(Having completed the "roads" on the rock face, he now turns to Bokkie.)

And many times when I am walking the roads looking for work I see . . . how do you say it . . . all the colors in the sky?

BOKKIE: It's a rainbow, Tata. Rainbow in the sky.

NUKAIN *(Relishing the word)*: Ewe, *rainbow*. When I walk the roads I see many rainbows in the sky. I say to myself that one day, you will also make a garden with flowers. So I walk, and walk, and walk, and one day I am walking down that road, and I come here to Vredewater . . . *(Pointing at the road at the bottom of the koppie)* . . . and I see Baas Hennie in front of the big house. I ask him if he has work for me. He asks me if I know how to fix fences and I say, yes, I do know how. So he gives me work for a day. Then another day . . . and another . . . and when he sees I do good work he takes me to an empty pondok and he tells me I can sleep there. And so it is. Then one day, here, I see another rainbow in the sky on top of this koppie, Bokkie. Special rainbow. It is so bright I close my eyes when I look at it. So that is when I know what I must do. So I go to the Baas and I tell him I want to make my own garden here. He looks at me and asks me why I want to make a garden with flowers, here where there is no water, and I tell him. I tell him it is not for flowers that drink water. I tell him I want to make rock flowers, I tell him about the rainbow I see at this koppie. And that is how it is. That is what I do all the time on Sundays . . . *(Looking around at his work)* But today, like last week . . . when I come here . . . I feel tired . . . moeg,

Bokkie, moeg, moeg, moeg. Because I try, but I can't find flowers inside me. The feeling in me is one I didn't know. But now I know what it was. Bring me all the colors, Bokkie.

(As Bokkie unloads the colors off the wagon, Nukain begins to paint a rainbow.

Bokkie watches the old man paint, handing him different colors as he calls for them. Eventually:)

BOKKIE: Yo! I can see your rainbow now, Tata. It's beautiful!
NUKAIN *(Looking at the completed painting)*: There. My story. Nukain Mabuza has told his story and there it is. And I am Man.

(Through all of the painting of the old man's story, Bokkie has taken in a vision of the old man and all that he has said. It is a vision that he will never forget.

Pause—a rich silence. Nukain sings quietly to himself—a fragment of a song that he has picked up on the road—as he makes his way to one of his "flowers," and sits down. Bokkie joins Nukain with the turpentine and a rag so that the old man can clean his hands. After a second or two more of silence between them, the old man makes a gentle but sweeping gesture that encompasses the wide landscape around them.)

Look, Bokkie. Look. Look everywhere. Is good! Is very good.
BOKKIE *(Looking around)*: Koppies. Lots of koppies, Tata.
NUKAIN: You know, Bokkie . . . I think there is a koppie for every man.
BOKKIE: For me also?

NUKAIN: Ja. When you are a man.

BOKKIE (*Looking around again and pointing in the distance*): I want that one.

NUKAIN: I don't think you can choose the one you want. But when you find him, Bokkie, you must do it.

BOKKIE: What, Tata? Paint it? Like this one?

NUKAIN: Maybe paint . . . maybe . . . Ja, maybe there is other work for you. Maybe you must do something else.

BOKKIE: But what, Tata? And when? Why must I . . .

NUKAIN: Why . . . why this . . . why that . . . there you do it again! No more whys for Tata, Bokkie. I only know what I must do. This koppie is for flowers, and the Big One for my story. I gave him all that I got. Now it is finished . . . now I got nothing more to give.

(*Elmarie enters humming "Aandgesang," a traditional Afrikaans hymn. She carries an enamel plate of food. The moment the old man and the boy see her, they break away from the shared intimacy of their moment alone and stand respectfully, waiting for her to speak. The old man doffs his cap. Bokkie watches as the pride and conviction that Nukain had achieved in telling his story slowly drain away.*)

ELMARIE: No, Outa, go on with what you were doing.

NUKAIN: No, no, Miesies Elmarie . . . we just talking.

ELMARIE: I brought you some food. I just thought you two might be hungry.

(*Bokkie steps forward to collect the plate of food. Elmarie reaches out to ruffle his hair playfully.*)

And you, Bokkie?

(Bokkie returns to Nukain's side.)

Have you forgotten how to say thank you?

BOKKIE *(After a nudge from Nukain)*: Thank you, Miesies.

ELMARIE: What's going on with you these days, klonkie?
You used to be such a polite little boy. It's high time
for you to teach this one some manners, Outa. Evelina
was complaining to me again this morning that he is
becoming very cheeky with her in the kitchen. Now don't
be greedy. Let Outa eat first.

　　(Looking at the summit rock for the first time) So, Outa,
you are busy now with this big one. But what is this now?
Is this now also supposed to be a flower? *(Perplexed by
what she sees, falteringly)* Where is the flower?

NUKAIN *(Turning to look at the big rock, he speaks
apologetically)*: Ag . . . just something, Miesies.

BOKKIE *(Has been watching and listening intently and cannot
contain himself)*: No, Tata! Tell the Miesies. *(Proudly)* It is
his story, Miesies. Tata's story.

ELMARIE: What does he mean, Outa?

NUKAIN: Ag, Miesies . . . Bokkie is also just talking . . .

BOKKIE: No! You know what it is, Tata. *(To Elmarie)* His
story is his life! Because he's got no more flowers inside.
Look, Miesies, this is Tata and all the roads he walked,
and the rainbows.

ELMARIE: No more flowers? What nonsense you are talking!
There are still plenty of rocks for more flowers. You've got
too many ideas in that small head of yours, Bokkie! Outa
doesn't need any new ideas. Heaven alone knows where
you get them from.

BOKKIE: It wasn't my idea . . .

ELMARIE: Passop, Bokkie. You must be careful.

(A rebuked Bokkie withdraws into sullen silence and sits down. With obvious concern, Elmarie turns to Nukain and speaks:)

You must keep an eye on him, Outa. Be strict, it's for his own good. If these children get too big for their shoes and start any nonsense here on the farm, the police will have to do what they did there in Johannesburg. Ja! I saw it on TV. Those skollies there in Soweto didn't want to go to school anymore, so they burnt down their classrooms and books. Too many strange ideas. If you ask me, it's the parents who are to blame for what happened up there. If those fathers had taken off their belts and given those schoolchildren a good hiding, none of that would have happened.

(Breaking away from Nukain and speaking as if thinking aloud:)

The Lord has been good to us here in Revolver Creek . . . Not so, Outa?

NUKAIN: Yes, Miesies.

(Elmarie goes up to the summit rock and studies it in silence for a few seconds. Then, shaking her head, she looks at the other smaller rocks with the colorful patterns. She nods her head appreciatively.)

ELMARIE: I was just a young woman when you started making your "flowers." Baas Hennie and I had just been married a year. Ja, I remember it like it was only yesterday. We were having Sunday lunch when you came to the back door and said you wanted to speak to him. When he came back to finish his food, he said that you had given him a little money and asked him to buy you some paint because you wanted to make flowers on the rocks of this koppie. You had wanted to thank the Lord for giving you work. Because I was curious, I came here next Sunday to see what you were doing. You were busy painting your second rock. Remember?

NUKAIN: Yes, Miesies. I remember. Because then later, the Miesies came and gave me back my money and said Miesies and Baas were going to buy paint for me.

ELMARIE *(Nodding her head and smiling in warm appreciation of the memory)*: Ja. That is how it was. And look at it now! You've done well, Outa.

(Looking out over the same view that Nukain did earlier. She is deeply moved by what she sees:)

We gave thanks in church today. Psalm 23.

(She recites Psalm 23 in Afrikaans:)

> Die Here is my herder; niks sal my ontbreek nie.
> Hy laat my neerlê in groen weivelde;
> na waters waar rus is, lei Hy my heen.
> Hy verkwik my siel.

Yes, that is how it is. He has led us beside still waters to green pastures. You know, Outa, when I look at the land like this I know what it feels like to be a mother, even though Baas Hennie and I haven't got children. Because at first we also wanted children . . . just like all the others. But then when it didn't happen, we realized that the good Lord had other plans for us, that our child was the land

and that we must look after it as our own blood. And look now . . . still waters and green pastures. Vredewater. Ja, so far the good Lord has kept our little world free of the trouble they are having in Johannesburg. We must all pray that he keeps that sort of trouble away from us here. Baas Hennie shakes his head when I tell him that. "The writing is on the wall," he says, "Have your guns ready as well as your Bible." That is what he believes.

(Rallying her convictions:)

But I don't believe him. The Lord won't let it come to that.

(Shaking herself out of her reverie, she sees Nukain's passbook at her feet. Picking it up, and realizing what it is, she hands it back to him.)

You dropped this again, Outa . . . mustn't be so careless. You know that it's important that you have this in your pocket all the time. Anyway . . . Outa, I must go now. We have got visitors coming this afternoon.

(Elmarie starts to leave. She stops and looks back at the rock. After a few moments of thought:)

Listen, Outa . . . do you want to do something for me?

NUKAIN: Ja, Miesies . . . anything.

ELMARIE *(Gesturing to the summit rock)*: Next Sunday . . . why don't you wipe all that away . . . and make this one a big flower, your biggest flower . . . to thank the Lord for all his blessings. *(Pause)* Did you hear me, Outa?

NUKAIN: Yes, Miesies.

BOKKIE *(Distressed by what he is hearing)*: But, Tata! It is your story.

ELMARIE *(Now losing her patience with Bokkie)*: What is this "story" nonsense he keeps going on about, Outa?

NUKAIN: Ag, Miesies . . . Bokkie is just talking.

BOKKIE: I'm not just talking! *(Defiantly)* You can't make him wipe it away!

ELMARIE *(Shocked by the little boy's effrontery)*: Excuse me?

BOKKIE *(Glancing at Nukain and faltering)*: I said, you can't make him . . .

ELMARIE *(Now very exasperated with Bokkie)*: Who do you think you're talking to? Evelina in the kitchen? *(Speaking sternly to Nukain)* Nee wragtig . . . I think it's time to take off your belt. I mean it, Outa. Teach him a lesson. You know the only way he will learn is through his backside. You hear me now. You took responsibility for him, so now it's time to take off your belt. I won't have a little klonkie with a head full of nonsense telling me what to do. *(To Bokkie)* Now bring that plate down to the kitchen when Outa is finished up here.

(She leaves.
Nukain and Bokkie stare at each other in silence, the latter struggling to contain the turbulent feelings inside him. He eventually looks at the old man and speaks with angry bitterness.)

BOKKIE: Why, Tata? Why?

NUKAIN: Why what?

BOKKIE: Us . . . *(Looking at the summit rock)* . . . that . . . Miesies . . . me . . . Tata! Why everything?

NUKAIN: What are you saying, Bokkie?

BOKKIE: Are you going to hit me, Tata?

NUKAIN: No, Bokkie. I won't hit you.

BOKKIE: Then why didn't you tell her it's your story? Don't wipe it away!

NUKAIN *(Shaking his head)*: Haai, Bokkie! You don't understand yet. If I don't wipe it away, then what? Miesies gets very cross with me and I lose my pondok? Lose my job? Look at me, Bokkie. What has Tata got? Nothing. I haven't even got a belt to hit you with. Not even that shack down there is mine. Even the old mattress I sleep on is not mine. Look at you. What has Bokkie got? A torn shirt and dirty short trousers. Now look at the Baas and the Miesies. What have they got? Everything! You heard the Miesies. The big house, the land, the cattle in the kraal, the fruit on the trees, the vegetables in the garden which Tata plants and waters. You see, Bokkie . . . they do not see us. Baas Hennie is a good baas, Miesies is a good miesies. But they are like the Big One before we give him eyes. They got eyes but they do not see us. There it is now . . . and Miesies wants me to wipe it away? Doesn't matter, Bokkie. Maybe one day Baas Hennie and Miesies Elmarie will open their eyes and then they will see us.

(Looking around wearily:)

Come, Bokkie.

(Nukain leaves. Bokkie stares at the rock for a little while longer, then collects the paints and brushes and loads them into the wagon. He spots the plate of food Elmarie brought them and picks it up. He hesitates and, on a sudden impulse, hurls it at the summit rock. He leaves, dragging the wagon behind him.)

ACT TWO

———

The same as Act One, except that it is now many years later. As a result of neglect during that time, the rocks are overgown with weeds. Rain and a harsh sun have left only traces of Nukain's original paintings. This is most noticeable in the case of the large summit rock.

Bokkie, now Jonathan Sejake, a young man in his early thirties, enters with his shoes tied around his neck. After surveying the scene, he makes his way to the rock where he and Nukain had sat together after painting the Big One. After a short rest, he leaves his backpack on the ground and makes his way to the summit rock. He is carefully tracing the outlines of Nukain's original painting when he hears Elmarie's voice from off. He immediately sits down near his backpack and tries to put on his shoes.

ELMARIE *(From off)*: Petrus? I've got somebody up here on old
Outa's hill . . . *(Crackle from a walkie-talkie and a muffled
voice: "Who is it?")* . . . He doesn't look like one of the
gang but phone the kommando just in case, and sommer
the police as well. I'll keep him here until they come . . .
(Another crackle and muffled voice: "I'll come and join you.")
No, you stay with Oubaas Hennie. I'll be all right.

*(She enters with a walkie-talkie in one hand and a handgun
in the other. She is obviously frightened but is doing her best
to hide it. Time has also left its mark on her. Her face has
settled into hard, bitter lines. Jonathan looks up to see Elmarie's gun pointed at him. Raising his hands in a defensive
gesture, he recognizes her immediately.)*

(Speaking to Jonathan, with her gun still pointed at him)
What are you doing here? This is private land.
JONATHAN *(Respectfully)*: I'm . . . I'm sorry. I tried the main
gate but it was locked. So I just climbed through the
fence . . . I noticed it was broken . . .
ELMARIE: Where? Where is it broken?
JONATHAN *(Pointing)*: Down there . . . just next to the old
windpump . . . where I've parked my car.
ELMARIE *(On her walkie-talkie again)*: Have you gotten
through to anybody yet? . . . *(A crackle from the walkie-
talkie and a muffled voice: "Not yet.")* . . . Then keep
trying. He got in through a hole in the fence next to the
road . . . near the old windpump. Just tell the kommando
when they arrive. *(Back to Jonathan)* So who are you?
What do you want? Are you alone?
JONATHAN: Mrs. Kleynhans? *(Pause)* You don't recognize me?
ELMARIE *(Surprised that he knows her name)*: Why should I?
JONATHAN: A long time ago you used to call me Bokkie.

ELMARIE *(Taken aback)*: You are . . .

JONATHAN: Yes, Mrs. Elmarie Kleynhans. That was me: Bokkie, the cheeky little helper of the old man you called Outa. *(Another pause)* You do at least still remember him, surely?

(For a moment she is thrown off-kilter by what he has said. After a few seconds she rallies and falls back into suspicion.)

ELMARIE: So what are you doing here? What do you want? *(She sees his backpack)* Is that yours?

JONATHAN: Yes.

ELMARIE: Open it.

JONATHAN: Why?

ELMARIE: Because I've got a gun and it's pointing at you.

JONATHAN: Are you threatening me?

ELMARIE: Yes I am.

(For a moment it looks as if he is going to refuse, but then thinks better of it, and unpacks the contents of his backpack.)

JONATHAN: Paint, Mrs. Kleynhans . . . black, yellow, green, white, blue, and red. The colors he used to make all his flowers.

ELMARIE: So?

JONATHAN *(Gesturing to the summit rock and all the others)*: I came here half hoping that someone would have cared enough about his Rock Garden to keep it as alive as it was when he painted that last rock. Still . . . I think there's enough of an outline of the original to go by.

ELMARIE: And you thought you could just come here and . . . and what? Paint it back?

JONATHAN: Yes. Restore it. I think that's the word people use.

ELMARIE *(Remembering him now, she lowers the gun)*: Still the cheeky little boy with a head full of nonsense.

JONATHAN: Yes, I think I remember you calling me that.

ELMARIE: So what gives you the right to come here and paint that rock without permission? Let me remind you, this is private property, Bokkie.

JONATHAN: Nobody calls me that anymore, Mrs. Kleynhans. My real name is Jonathan Sejake.

ELMARIE: You haven't changed much.

(On her walkie-talkie again) Is anybody on their way yet? . . . *(Again, a crackle on the walkie-talkie and a muffled response: "No, still nothing.")* . . . Then don't try again . . . and if they call you just say . . . *(She hesitates, but after looking at Jonathan, speaks again)* . . . just say it was a false alarm . . . *(Another crackle and a muffled voice: "Are you all right?")* . . . Ja, I'm fine . . . it's just someone I used to know.

(Elmarie switches off the walkie-talkie.)

JONATHAN: Violating your property rights is not one of my "strange ideas," Mrs. Kleynhans. Our new constitution protects your rights . . . as it now also does mine.

ELMARIE: Then tell that to those four black brothers of yours who attacked the Potgieters night before last. They didn't only ransack the house, they also brutalized and tortured that innocent old couple. Mr. Potgieter is dead, a pitchfork through his neck, and Mrs. Potgieter is lying in the intensive care unit in hospital, so bruised she can't even open her eyes . . . her whole body covered with cigarette burns. And all because she couldn't remember the code for the safe! The doctors don't expect her to live.

(She sits down wearily on a rock.)

JONATHAN (*Shocked*): The Potgieters? At Onverwacht?

ELMARIE: You remember them?

JONATHAN: Yes. I remember them very clearly. They certainly didn't deserve that. They were good people . . .

ELMARIE: Of course they were.

JONATHAN (*Shaking his head in disbelief*): They used to let us children into their orchard when the fruit was ripe.

ELMARIE: And where did their generosity get them? May God help us catch the black bastards who did this. Everybody is out there searching for them.

JONATHAN: Black bastards? That's what hunger and desperation . . . and anger has done to many of us black people.

ELMARIE (*Outraged*): What are you saying? Are you trying to excuse what they did? Do you expect me to have feelings for them now as well? This is the fourth farm attack this month!

JONATHAN: At least try to understand . . .

ELMARIE (*Cutting him short*): Never! It makes no difference what kind of life those men came from, what they did was absolutely unforgivable.

(*A pause as she fights back the tears that suddenly overwhelm her.*)

Onverwacht! There's a bitter taste now to the name of that farm. Oom Flippie and Ouma Bessie certainly weren't expecting those midnight visitors they woke up to find in their bedroom.

JONATHAN (*Softly, shaking his head despairingly*): Please, Mrs. Kleynhans, don't misunderstand me. The Potgieters most certainly did not deserve what happened to them.

ELMARIE: Of course not! They were good, God-fearing people . . . as are most of us Afrikaner farmers. And as for those four men, all they deserve is to have a rope put around their necks and dropped into the Hell that is waiting for them. But that won't happen anymore. This is mos now your "New South Africa" with its . . . *(Bitter irony)* "wonderful constitution." So they will live on.

(Pause.)

JONATHAN *(Giving up)*: I won't bother you anymore, Mrs. Kleynhans. This is obviously not the right moment. I'll go now . . . but just so that you know, I had every intention of going to your house and asking Mr. Kleynhans and you for permission to restore the painting on that rock.

ELMARIE *(Shaking her head)*: You'd be wasting your breath, yet again. Mr. Kleynhans can't speak anymore. He had a stroke a few months ago. He can't even walk properly now. If you want permission you only have to ask me, Mr. . . . whatever you want me to call you now.

(He ignores her gibe and, after taking a deep breath, steadies himself and tries yet again:)

JONATHAN: Then I am asking you, Mrs. Kleynhans, do I have your permission to restore Nukain Mabuza's last painting?

(Elmarie shakes her head in disbelief.)

Yes. He also had a real name.

(Pause.)

So do I have your permission to restore it?

ELMARIE: But why?

(She looks at the summit rock.)

Can you remember what it looked like? It wasn't covered
with beautiful patterns like all the others he painted.

JONATHAN: I remember very clearly what it looked like.
I was here with him, remember . . . *(He can't keep a note of
bitterness out of his voice)* . . . when you asked him to scrub
it away and "make one last big flower to thank the good
Lord"—if I remember correctly—"for all his blessings."

ELMARIE: I just wish he had lived for one more Sunday so
that he could have done that. That is what that poor old
man deserved, one last big flower. But instead . . . *(At a
loss for words)* . . . instead of that, he painted . . . what did
you call it, his "story"! Isn't that what you called it?

JONATHAN: Yes . . . that is what it was. His story.

ELMARIE: I've often wondered . . . was it you who put the
idea in his head that he must now do something different?

JONATHAN: No, he surprised me as well.

ELMARIE: His story! We've all got stories. What was so
special about his?

*(He goes to the summit rock and looks at it, then turns and
talks to Elmarie:)*

JONATHAN: Try to imagine, Mrs. Kleynhans, what it was
like for a black man or woman in this country to reach
the end of their life—because that is where he was on
that Sunday—with nothing to show for it? When he died
three days later, lying alone down there in his pondok,
I wasn't really surprised. He was old, and tired and

frightened. Frightened, because in spite of all the flowers he had painted, in spite of having, as he once said, "the most beautiful garden in the whole world," he wasn't fulfilled. You see, Mrs. Kleynhans, my black brothers and sisters really are, as you Afrikaners claim to be, the children of this land. They have watered this earth with their sweat and tears and walked all the roads in this country looking for work . . . "the black roads," as Nukain used to call them. But what do they have to show for it?

ELMARIE: And do you think we Afrikaners haven't also watered this land with our sweat and our tears? Read the history book, Mr. . . .

JONATHAN: Sejake, Mrs. Kleynhans. Jonathan Sejake . . .

ELMARIE: Be patient with me . . . Mr. Sejake . . . I will learn your name.

(She takes a small, well-thumbed, and obviously old Bible out of her pocket.)

It sounds as if you have read many books since I last saw you, but do you know this one? It was my grandmother's Bible. Read the Book of Job and then you might understand something about us Afrikaners. For us, this book is the source of all wisdom, the foundation of our faith. It has guided my people for centuries. Given us hope and courage in the darkest of times . . . and for us Afrikaners this is certainly one of the darkest.

(Pause.)

Our entire little community was in church this morning. Everyone there knew and loved the Potgieters, Oom

Flippie and Ouma Bessie. Our hearts were heavy with bitterness and grief. Dominee Badenhorst knew that, so he read to us from the Book of Job and urged us to think about that moment when Job cried out to the Lord: "Aarde, moenie my bloed bedek nie, en laat daar geen rusplek vir my geroep wees nie!" . . . "Earth, do not cover up my blood, do not hide it, and let there be no resting place for my cry!" That is what we Afrikaners are crying out now. You know, young man, I used to come here and look out over Vredewater and feel good, feel blessed. Not just because we owned it, Mr. Sejake, but because we belonged. We are rooted in it like the oldest of the thorn trees down there by the stream. Now there are days when I feel I don't belong here anymore. But where can I go? Then, I feel that bitter cry of Job's is also ours . . . that the blood of my people, of the Potgieters, and the hundreds of others who have been brutalized and murdered on their farms, will end up covered up and forgotten. How many more Afrikaners must be murdered before this country wakes up and realizes it is all part of a deliberate plan to drive us Afrikaners off our land! Yes! A deliberate plan, and nobody is doing anything about it.

(Pause.)

I know that a loss of faith is a big sin, and I am ashamed to say that I have been guilty of it quite a few times lately. It happened again after the attack on the Potgieters. These times are a severe challenge to our faith. But I prayed for forgiveness in church this morning, and I know the Lord is merciful and that He will forgive me . . .

(Pause.)

When the first Kleynhans outspanned his ox wagon down there in 1849—more than a hundred and fifty years ago—where our house is now, this land was a wilderness. Look at it now. We tamed it, made it feed people. When your Tata came to us all those years ago and said he was looking for work, he was thin, starving. He was in rags. We fed him. We gave him work. Mr. Kleynhans pulled some of his old clothes out of the cupboard and gave them to him, and when we saw that he was a good worker, Mr. Kleynhans showed him an empty pondok where he could make his home. But believe me, young man, if I woke up in the middle of the night and found him in my house, I would pick up my gun and I would shoot. Yes, I mean it. If I find him standing in front of me like that rock, I will not think twice, I will point this gun and I will shoot . . .

(She impulsively raises her gun, takes aim at the rock, and is on the point of pulling the trigger when Jonathan intervenes.)

JONATHAN *(Jumping forward and standing directly in the line of fire, between her and the rock)*: Go on! Shoot! Pull the trigger!

(Both of them freeze. Elmarie lowers the gun. Jonathan slumps to the ground at the base of the rock.)

ELMARIE *(Very shaken by what nearly happened)*: Are you mad? I could have killed you.

JONATHAN: Yes. If your bullet was meant for him then I would have claimed it instead.

(Pause.)

On that last Sunday of his life, he couldn't stand up here as you did and look out proudly over *his* land. All he had left in him, in his life, was what he painted on that rock. That rock is his—the only thing he could claim at the end of his life.

ELMARIE *(Flaring up again)*: "Claim"? That rock is on our land. It is ours.

JONATHAN *(No longer able to contain his anger)*: Your land?

ELMARIE: Oh, I see. You want to be like Mugabe and his bunch up in Zimbabwe. Look at the state that country is in now. It can't even feed its own people anymore.

JONATHAN: Yes. I do believe in taking back the land. But it doesn't have to end like that. Anyway, don't worry, Mrs. Kleynhans. At the moment, our constitution safeguards your right to your stolen land.

ELMARIE: Well, you should be grateful we "stole" it. Because look what we have done with it. All your Tata's "black roads" were built by us.

(Shaking her head with a bitter smile) Anyway, you don't seem to have much faith in your new constitution, do you? "At the moment" . . .

JONATHAN *(Losing his temper)*: To hell with the constitution. Protecting the land rights of whites was a compromise that should never have happened. When the time comes, as it will, we will change it and Nukain can take back from you his story.

(A pause as he fights back his tears.)

ELMARIE *(Unrelenting)*: Tonight, when I get into bed next to Mr. Kleynhans, I will read to him from the Bible, aloud, because I know he and the Almighty can hear me. Then I will close it and put it down on my bedside table . . .

next to this gun. And make no mistake, I won't care who stands in front of me in the middle of the night, I will pull the trigger and shoot . . . even if it was your beloved Tata . . . or you. Oh yes. We also don't need the constitution. We will fight to protect ourselves and what is rightfully ours.

JONATHAN (*Another flare of anger*): Stop calling him Tata, or Outa, or anything else! He had a real name, Mrs. Kleynhans. It is on his grave in Barberton. Have you seen his grave?

ELMARIE: Yes I have.

JONATHAN: Well then you know that it says: "Nukain Mabuza, Died in 1981," and then the passbook number, that hated dompas number, that your government made all us black people carry.

ELMARIE: Just so that you know, Mr. Sejake, we paid for that grave. Oh yes. We Afrikaners are not the merciless "boers" you all want to shoot . . . "Kill the farmer, kill the boer"—that's the war cry these days, isn't it? We paid for it because we cared. Our consciences demanded that he have a proper grave. So we handed his body and his passbook over to the police, together with money for the grave.

(*A helpless gesture. Overwhelmed for the moment by a sense of defeat, he packs the tins of paint back into his backpack and starts to leave. After a few seconds, he stops and looks at Elmarie. He hesitates, then sits down on one of the rocks closest to him.*)

JONATHAN: Come on, Mrs. Kleynhans, let us try again.

ELMARIE: Try what?

JONATHAN: Try to understand each other. If we can't do that . . . then one thing is certain: our future will be as big a mess as anything in our past.

ELMARIE: You think you understand me?

JONATHAN: You don't make it easy for me, but I am trying.

ELMARIE: And how far have you got, Mr. Sejake?

JONATHAN: You are an Afrikaner, and I have a sense, whether you are conscious of it or not, that you subscribe to that central belief of the Afrikaner mythology that you are a chosen people, and that your mission . . .

(Elmarie is shaking her head. He stops.)

What?

ELMARIE *(Losing her aggressive edge, suddenly frightened and old)*: It is so much simpler than that. I am also a woman, just a frightened white woman. Do you know what that feels like?

JONATHAN *(Stopped short)*: No.

(Pause.)

Do you know what it feels like when the only person who you love, and who loves you, is ordered to beat you . . . and all because the white Miesies is feeling challenged? Remember?

(Elmarie stares at him with disbelief.)

You told Nukain to take off his belt. I can still feel the welts on my backside from the lashing that I never got. Do you know what that feels like?

ELMARIE: No. *(Pause)* But I do know that I am trying to understand that our little Bokkie has grown up to become Mr. Jonathan Sejake.

JONATHAN: On that last Sunday, when you came up here with a plate of leftovers for the two of us, and were so dismissive of what you saw on the rock, I tried to tell you what it was all about. Remember? I tried to tell you that it was his story. You see, Nukain and what he painted on that rock changed my life. Yes. Changed my life. I didn't come here today to indulge in a few sad memories of him. For all I know, I might well have ended up as one of those "black bastards" who broke into the Potgieters' house. Yes, I mean that. But instead . . .

(For a moment he is at a loss for words. Eventually:)

Have you ever seen a man stand up after a lifetime of humiliation and claim his dignity as a human being? I saw it happen that day. At the very end of his life, Nukain stood up . . . stood there! And in a final act of rebellion against the society in which he lived and the all-loving God you all believe in, he claimed his dignity as a man. Not an old man. Not as a black man. But simply as a man. And in doing that, standing right there with his tired old body and white hair, he challenged me in a way that I know now will stay with me until the day I die.

ELMARIE: Then why did you run away from it? When you disappeared, we did everything we could to try to find you. Mr. Kleynhans stopped work on the farm and sent the boys out in every direction to try to find you and bring you back home.

JONATHAN: Home? Home? Revolver Creek was never my home, Mrs. Kleynhans. I ran away because Revolver Creek had become a place of disgrace, of humiliation.

(Pause.)

When Nukain finished painting the Big One—that is what we called it—we sat here side by side, for a few precious moments, basking in the warmth of knowing that a good thing had happened. But then . . . *(Shaking his head)* . . . you appeared, and the moment he saw you he reverted—in an instant!—to being once again just one of your "boys" . . . just another servile old "kaffer." Young as I was, my sense of betrayal was more than I could cope with. *(With a bitter smile)* At that moment, the only way I could think of promising myself that it would never, never, happen to me was to throw away that plate of leftovers you had brought for us.

ELMARIE: So?

JONATHAN: I avoided him after that, and three days later when we found him dead in his pondok . . . I cried. But all I could think of was that big rock, the Big One, of how proudly defiant he had stood in front of it and said: *"I am Man!"* And I had this sense that Nukain had left it to me . . . but I didn't want it. I was frightened of it just as Nukain himself had been frightened of it until he confronted it. I couldn't live here on the farm with that rock up here, challenging me every day.

(Pause.)

So . . . yes, I ran away. I slept on the side of the road that first night. The next day, I carried on walking "the black

roads." They had led Nukain to Revolver Creek, but in
my case they carried me away . . . far away. When I came
to the border and they refused to let me pass because I had
nothing to show, no dompas, nothing, they laughed at
me, taunted me: "Go back to you mother, little boy." . . .
And chased me away. All I had was my desire, my need
to get as far away from this place as my legs could carry
me. I never once thought about coming back. So I found
ways of going forward: crawling under barbed-wire fences
in the middle of the night, hiding away on the back
of lorries, the trucks of freight trains . . . anything that
would take me further.

(Pause.)

My journey ended in Harare. Yes, Harare. They were
good to me there. You see, those people were free.
Mugabe had won them their freedom and they had grown
strong and generous feeding on it. When I told them
where I had come from, they understood, because, as you
no doubt know, your proud and defiant young Republic
was greatly despised in the outside world. So they fed me
until I could find work and feed myself. And when they
saw that I wanted to educate myself, they helped me do
that. Now I can read, I can write. I am a teacher and
I want to teach other young people. I want to empower
young South Africans to find their rightful place in this
new South Africa. But in all that time, I never forgot the
Big One. It lived on with me. Until gradually, I realized
that one day I would have to face it just as Nukain
had done. But then, what really frightened me was the
thought that when I returned, I would find that you had
scrubbed it away as you had wanted Nukain to do.

(He picks up a small stone at his feet and plays with it for a few seconds.)

Do you know how many flowers he painted? I tried to count them for him one day. If I remember correctly, the number was one hundred and five. I am sure it was much more than that, but that was the number I came up with that day. I was only eleven years old, remember. By the time he painted the Big One, it was one hundred and eight. You see, Mrs. Kleynhans, that last painting of his, that you so despised, is a remarkable achievement. You should be proud of it. An illiterate old "native" told his story for others to read in the only language he knew.

(Now looking squarely at her.)

If he had been alive that next Sunday, would you really have told him to scrub it away?

ELMARIE *(Evasively)*: That was all a long time ago.

JONATHAN *(Studying Elmarie for a few more seconds before speaking)*: Come on, Mrs. Kleynhans, we are talking honestly to each other. Would you have told him to do it? You were very insistent that Sunday afternoon.

ELMARIE *(Reluctantly)*: I don't know. Maybe. But as it turned out, his death, just three days after he had painted that rock, had a strange effect on me. I was sad for his sake and I of course prayed for him, but there was also something else. I don't know . . . there was something else . . . that strange thing he had painted on the rock and all your talk about "his story." That next Sunday I came up here to look at it. What I do know, is I meant to scrub it away. I had a bottle of turpentine and a scrubbing brush. I meant to do it.

(Pause.)

But . . . somehow . . . I just couldn't. I knew that if I just left it alone, God's rain and sunshine would do it . . . as it nearly has.

JONATHAN: So I came back just in time. A month ago, in fact. You see, as the years passed I had settled deeper and deeper into my life in Zimbabwe. I had a home in Harare, books and music on shelves. I was of course watching South Africa all the time. Like my fellow exiles, I knew the change would come. And then one day on the television screen I saw Nelson Mandela walking out of jail after twenty-seven years of imprisonment. What I hadn't expected, however, was the homesickness. Instead of the comfortable little ache that I had grown used to, it now sprang into violent life and savaged me . . . day in and day out. And the memories! Your voice, Mrs. Kleynhans . . . yes, yours! Talking Afrikaans to Mr. Kleynhans on the stoep in the late afternoon when I was weeding your flower bed. Yes! Believe it or not, it became one of my most cherished memories. Back there in Harare, I even started talking Afrikaans to myself! And then smells . . . the memory of smells . . . Nukain's sweaty body after a long day of hard work, the horseshoe tobacco that he rolled into newspaper zols, the salty taste of my tears when he died. It became too much. And by then, as you know, that fat Zimbabwe that I first encountered had become thin. Mugabe the great liberator was turning into Mugabe the monster. So here I am. I arrived in Barberton a month ago. I am the new principal of the high school there. I do not have a vision of flowers. I love language the way he loved color. And I know I am still too young to have a story to tell like him. But maybe one day when

I am a lot older I will tell it, on the pages of a book. I will use my pen and the English language, just as Nukain used his brush and tins of paint. But first, I must bring his story back to life.

(Jonathan goes to the rock and once again traces the outline of Nukain's painting. Turning to face Elmarie:)

So I ask you again, Mrs. Kleynhans . . . do I have your permission to restore Nukain Mabuza's last painting?

(He waits for an answer. Elmarie and Jonathan stare unflinchingly at each other.)

ELMARIE *(Quietly)*: You have my permission.

(Jonathan, softly singing the work song "We Majola" that Nukain had taught him before, takes off his shirt and tie, revealing a vest underneath. He fetches his backpack and unpacks the paints and brushes. Turning to Elmarie:)

JONATHAN: Walking or working, you must sing, Bokkie!

(He moves to where Nukain had stood when he confronted the summit rock. Elmarie watches him.
    Jonathan's voice is charged with excitement:)

Yes! This is where he stood and said: "Give him eyes, Bokkie!" . . . And he held out the brush to me. I had helped him paint a few of the small rocks, and I had fun doing it, but this time I suddenly felt frightened. He was a Tata I had never seen before . . . fierce and angry and commanding. I tried to say no, but he insisted: "Do it, Bokkie! Give him eyes."

(Using black-and-white paint, Jonathan restores the eyes of the Big One. As he does so, he sings again, this time with more volume and conviction. When he is finished, he goes back to the spot where Nukain had stood.)

Yes! Now you see me . . . And I am Man!

(Elmarie is watching him carefully as the lights fade to black.)

END OF PLAY

Afterthought

On Joules and on Creativity

By Paula Fourie

In his introduction to the 2013 revised edition of *Angels in America*, Tony Kushner asks us, "Should plays have introductions?"[1] Despite going on to write one, he thinks not. Like Herman Melville's Ishmael, Kushner instead invites the reader to jump in cold, to "plunge in without preparation." If the playwright has constructed a raft solid enough, so the thinking presumably goes, his or her audience should be able to trust that they will survive the ocean voyage. Altered, of course, but very much alive. Athol Fugard would surely agree. He has often told me that to write a play is no different from building a table. It needs, first and foremost, sturdy legs, and equipped thus by its loving maker, will be able to stand on its own four feet.

It is right, then, that the audience of this slim volume not be confronted with anything before Bokkie and Nukain scramble up their koppie, the former jumping from rock to rock like his namesake; the latter, a little bit tired. But what about the fact that that same koppie is at least a thousand miles away from any theater where *The Painted Rocks at Revolver Creek* has been staged, that the play is set in an entirely different world than is known by most of its readers? I can only answer that the koppie in question is not in fact anywhere but in the mind of Athol Fugard, an equally remote world, yes, but one surely served best by the map he himself has already chosen to provide for it. Unlike the vast majority of places where Fugard has chosen to set his plays, he has never once been to the stone garden of Nukain Mabuza in Barberton, Mpumalanga, from whence he drew the inspiration for this, his latest play.

When Athol asked me, as someone who had witnessed the writing of *The Painted Rocks at Revolver Creek* and who had been involved in two stagings of it, to write some text to accompany the published play, I decided that what I wanted to offer instead of an introduction was an afterthought. Useful, perhaps, only because none of us has been to Nukain's garden, and very few to Fugard's desk or rehearsal room. Necessary, I believe, because the sheer energy (how does one measure energy, in joules?) expended and refracted across time by all the characters involved in the creation of this play, including Athol Fugard, deserves to be reckoned with. Herewith, then, the attempt at an accounting.

This play has its origins in *Visions*, a short one-act play written by Fugard in response to what he calls "my fascination with the vision that drives seemingly ordinary human beings to create something totally unique, whose creativity operates outside of orthodoxy."[2] Years earlier, the South African artist Paul Stopforth had drawn Fugard's attention to outsider artist Nukain Mabuza, whose life and work became an important inspiration for the play. Completed in 2008, *Visions* already featured as characters the artist and the young helper Fugard had given him, Bokkie. Of course, the term "visionary environment" is generally recognized as one of the manifestations of outsider art, where individuals obsessively transform their immediate environments in a highly individualistic way. "Such environments," John Maizels writes in his book *Raw Creation: Outsider Art and Beyond*, "represent one of the most extraordinary forms of human creativity."[3] Mabuza's work is a recognized example of this phenomenon, having been featured in Maizels's book already in 1996 as an example of such a visionary environment.

When Fugard finally went in search of Mabuza in the mid-2000s, he found a wealth of photographs of his work and research about him online. That his legacy had been kept alive at all until then is thanks to yet another South African artist, JFC Clarke, as well as to the many individuals that he acknowledges in his own book, *The Painted Stone Garden of Nukain Mabuza* (2013). Although Fugard had begun to write Nukain well before this book was published, Clarke had been photographing Mabuza's work and conducting biographical research on the man since the 1980s. He had curated an exhibition at the Pretoria Art Museum in 1992 titled *The Stones Revisited*, and had by 2001 published shorter texts on Mabuza as well.[4] Fugard did not have to go to Revolver Creek to reimagine the painted rocks that he would eventually put on the stage, nor would he have found much there. As Clarke writes in 2013, "Revolver Creek has changed, the world has moved on and the original Stone Garden has all but disappeared."[5]

In early 2014, having been given a slot to present a new play at the Signature Theatre by its beloved artistic director, the late Jim Houghton, Fugard dug through his bottom drawer to find *Visions*, the outline and basic setting of which soon became the first act of a longer play. At the time of writing this miniature one-act, Fugard had been a resident of Southern California. He had since returned to South Africa, and as artist-in-residence at the Stellenbosch Institute for Advanced Study (STIAS) from September to December 2014, conceived what he would call *The Painted Rocks at Revolver Creek*.

In Stellenbosch, Fugard crafted a first act, now including the character of Elmarie Kleynhans. He then began writing a second, set some twenty years later in a South Africa more contemporary than anything he had written before. One of the inspirations for this second act and, in particular, Elmarie's cry: "Aarde, moenie my bloed bedek nie, en laat daar geen rusplek vir my geroep wees nie!" [Earth, do not cover up my blood, do not hide it, and let there be no resting place for my cry!], was a book that Fugard picked up in the little shop attached to the Stellenbosch Botanical Gardens. Titled *Treurgrond: 20 Jaar van Plaasaanvalle in Suid-Afrika [Land of Sorrows: 20 Years of Farm Attacks in South Africa]*, it was published in 2011 by Kraal Uitgewers, perhaps appropriately, though most likely incidentally, situated on the corner of DF Malan and Eendracht Streets in Pretoria.[6]

White farm murders in contemporary South Africa constitute a highly charged political narrative of claims to exclusive victimhood on the one hand, and a refutation of the vulnerability and patterns of violence that have emerged after apartheid, on the other. Articulating the former, *Treurgrond* documents the date, place and manner of death of the 2,617 individuals, mainly white farmers and their families, who have been murdered on South African farms between 1990 and 2010. Fugard was instantly drawn to and shocked by the individual human deaths chronicled in the book as well as by the sermon delivered at its end by Dr. A. L. A. Buys. Soon the discovery of *Treurgrond* revealed itself as one of the many "accidents" that have peppered Fugard's writing for more than six decades, seemingly chance events or encounters that have influenced whatever he was writing at the time.

Fugard completed *The Painted Rocks at Revolver Creek* in February 2015 in his little den in Sneeuberg Lodge, the big red-roofed house in the Karoo village of Nieu-Bethesda that was, at that time, our home. It is the same village that was once home to Helen Martins, that other outsider artist who had captured Fugard's imagination some thirty years earlier when he wrote *The Road to Mecca* (1984), and he had written many plays there. But the labor of that day and of the preceding months, "the inquisition of blank paper," as he calls it, had taken its toll on the then eighty-three-year-old Fugard. The morning after he sent off a rehearsal-room script to the Signature Theatre in New York City, he woke up with a severely strained neck. Later that day, he fainted in the little hallway separating the bathroom from the kitchen (let me just say that old Karoo houses are constructed in inexplicable ways). And although I managed to catch him and break his fall, after several minutes I finally had to lay him down as best I could, one leg bent underneath his body like the crushed spider he had once found on the steps of STIAS.

After friends from down the road (the couple who own Dustcovers, Athol's favorite bookshop) came to help, I rushed Athol off to the doctor. But getting to the nearest medical help is to undertake a winding drive of forty-five minutes, part of it on a dirt road and part of it through a mountain pass, to the town of Graaff-Reinet. And then there are the kudus, the largest of the South African antelopes. Athol is always warning me about the kudus jumping across the road, reminding me that the wife of a farmer friend of his ended up paralyzed because she had crashed into one with her car. Athol revived a couple of minutes into the journey, tried to convince me to turn around, but eventually resigned himself to join me in looking out for kudus jumping across the road. Having arrived safely in Graaff-Reinet, he was seen by a doctor who soon judged that his fainting spell had something to do with the heat of a Karoo summer, but more with taking a strong prescription painkiller Athol had brought with him from America, the kind of pill, so the doctor said, that you should really take lying down.

We laughed about that last observation. But there was no denying the shock and fear underneath our hilarity. I think we knew then that we had both underestimated the energy that would be required to turn *Visions* into *The Painted Rocks at Revolver Creek* in the short months that followed on two different productions of his previous play, *The Shadow of the Hummingbird*. 2014 had been a busy year. Fugard had played the main character, Oupa, in both New Haven and in Cape Town, his in-ear-monitor wired to the microphone in my hand during each performance in case he needed help remembering his lines.

After Athol's visit to the doctor that February 2015, we treated ourselves to a Sunday lunch in town, then returned to Nieu-Bethesda, still looking out for Kudus. And as we passed through the stubby dry landscape, I remembered what Athol had told me some years earlier, the very first time we had driven through the Karoo together: "You see those little gwarrie trees?" he had asked. "Underneath each of them is a story waiting to be told."

In his book, *The Painted Stone Garden of Nukain Mabuza* (2013), JFC Clarke draws on several newspaper articles and interviews with those who knew the man to sketch what little is known about his life. With grateful thanks to Clarke, the bare bones of Mabuza's life are retold here:

Those who knew Mabuza from his time at Revolver Creek believe him to have grown up in or near the Mozambican town of Moamba, not too far from the South African border. He is understood to have belonged to the "Shangaan-Tsonga" ethnic group, and, ostensibly following one of his married sisters, traveled from Mozambique to South Africa in the 1950s in search of work. He is thought to have landed up on a number of other farms near Barberton in Mpumalanga before finally being employed at Esperado in 1965, a farm near the Revolver Creek railway siding. This is the farm on which Mabuza would create his stone garden.

As a laborer on Esperado, established practice allowed him to join the other workers in making a home for himself on a part of the farm, however temporary it may turn out to be. Mabuza erected two huts at the base of a hill that overlooked the road between the towns of Barberton and Kaapmuiden. There he spent the next fifteen years decorating his home, painting his huts, the rocks in his yard, and the boulders and smaller rocks stretching up the hill. Mabuza would have earned very little as a farm worker employed to water vegetables and make tomato boxes, but as he was unmarried and had no dependants, could spend his money on the paint and brushes he used for his striking geometric designs. While he used his wages, his employer, Guido Fontana, would often bring him the paint he needed from Barberton or from the nearby city of Nelspruit.

Soon, tourists and other travelers through the district began to stop at Mabuza's home to admire his work. In response, he expanded his garden and orientated its layout toward the public road. Often, they would give him donations or gifts, and so he was able to buy even more paint. Clarke writes that "he painted obsessively, whenever he had an opportunity and slowly the size of his garden increased."[7] Sometimes, Nukain paid young people from the community to help him clear the bush around his rocks. Sometimes, they also helped him to paint. By the early 1970s, he began adding pictograms of animals to his garden, a crucifix, and what is thought to have been a self-portrait: "A thick, partially dotted line described a standing figure holding what could be a paintbrush. There was no attempt at a likeness."[8] By the mid-1970s, Mabuza's home and his garden had become an important tourist attraction, a landmark in the area. It was in these years that René Lion-Cachet, a representative from a fertilizer company who had taken an interest in Mabuza's work over the years, approached a shop in Nelspruit and arranged for a donation of paint. This changed Mabuza's life, enabling him to abandon his farm work entirely and live out the decade as full-time artist. In the year 1976, he fantastically claimed to have been a hundred years old. Writing in the *Farmer's Weekly* magazine, Lion-Cachet estimated him closer to sixty.

Nukain Mabuza's ending reads as mysteriously as his life. In 1979 or 1980, still ostensibly in good health, he announced that he had grown tired of life and that he intended to dig his own grave. When the other farm workers complained that it would violate local custom if Mabuza were buried next to his huts, it was decided in consultation with the landowners that he should be buried elsewhere. In response, Mabuza demolished his huts, defaced his paintings by smearing brown paint over them, and left, moving in the ensuing year from one farm to the next. He committed suicide in October 1981 on the farm Greenstone. Clarke concludes his biographical sketch of Mabuza by noting that he was buried in an unmarked grave in the Barberton Emjindini cemetery.

There are of course a great many differences between the Nukain of Fugard's play and the Mabuza of Clarke's research, and these are not limited to his tender relationship with Bokkie or the fraught yet familiar one with Elmarie. Fugard frequently stresses that he is not a biographer, that he cannot impose the constraints of lived experience on his imagination; instead, as in *The Road to Mecca*, he has chosen to freely reimagine the artist's life and the life of those around him or her. Feeling that he had strayed too far from what was known about the historical Mabuza, Fugard has always been cautious about using his name, of pertinently identifying him as a character in the play. In *Visions,* as well as in early drafts of *The Painted Rocks at Revolver Creek,* the old man is known simply as "Tata," a respectful form of address to a father or older man in the Xhosa language that says more about his relationship with Bokkie than it serves to identify him outside of it. Fugard's manuscripts only went as far as to acknowledge that what he had written was "suggested by the life and work of Nukain Mabuza."

Yet in February 2015, Fugard finally decided that he had no choice but to name his character Nukain Mabuza and to give him a tombstone with his name on it, something that the real man never had. I believe that he finally realized, no matter how differently he had written Nukain, that not to do so would be to commit an act of grave violence to the man and his memory. For, in as far as it exists, I believe that Fugard has captured and put onto the stage a core truth of Mabuza's life: that as a black man in apartheid South Africa forced to live on land that he could never legally own, he had to claim it through other means—by inscribing his very life on its granite boulders.

Just as the creative artist is a familiar figure in Fugard's work, so too is the basic arc of two individuals making the journey toward understanding; reaching a reconciliation of sorts even if it means simply reconciling themselves to each other. Consider Morris and Zachariah in *The Blood Knot* (1961), for example, or Gideon le Roux and Martinus Zoeloe in *Playland* (1993). Embedded in these journeys is Fugard's conviction that understanding engenders empathy, that telling stories can heal. As Morris says to Zachariah, "Talking helps, doesn't it?" Frequently, these journeys also embody Fugard's hope for reconciliation in

South Africa, his belief that the central arena of human history is there when two individuals confront each other.

In Fugard's Act Two, it is Jonathan Sejake and Elmarie Kleynhans who inhabit this arena. Jonathan at first appearing as a sort of "magic negro," then as the act progresses, discarding this guise to speak truth to power. But, although he alludes to a time in the future when land expropriation without compensation will take place, he stops short of violating Elmarie's land rights himself. Ultimately, his respect for the new South African constitution informs all of his behavior, leading to a show of extraordinary patience toward Elmarie, and not only because she has a gun. That Act Two takes place in the early 2000s is significant—the era of Nelson Mandela and all that he was seen to symbolize was already fading. But that Fugard completed this play just before South Africa was gripped by the Fallist movement is perhaps even more significant. Jonathan straddles these eras, in his words the portent that the politics of reconciliation were beginning to give away to those of decoloniality. *The Painted Rocks at Revolver Creek,* Fugard's first play since returning to live in the country of his birth, is his attempt to join the urgent conversation around the issue of land redistribution, key if we are ever to meaningfully address the inequality that continues to pervade South African society.

Then again, Fugard's plays have never been about ideas. They are about people, flesh-and-blood characters whose behavior onstage is governed only by who they are. The climax of the second act is not when Elmarie pulls her gun on Nukain's painting and Jonathan jumps into the line of fire, nor when he, incapable of restraint, finally exclaims, "To hell with the constitution. Protecting the land rights of whites was a compromise that should never have happened." Instead, it is in the raw exchange between the two after he sits down to urge her, "Come on, Mrs. Kleynhans, let us try again." It is when the two characters, stripped of their respective ideologies, try to put themselves in each other's shoes; Jonathan faced with Elmarie's debilitating fear, she by his sense of powerlessness, the loss of black self-determination effected by her own behavior and that of her fellow white South Africans.

It is fitting that no conclusive reconciliation, no forgiving embrace, is possible between the two. It remains out of reach, perhaps reflecting Fugard's own disillusionment in the post-post-apartheid era, his own misgivings over whether the Truth and Reconciliation Commission achieved what it set out to do, and his growing sense of doubt over the possibility of a non-racial and peaceful South Africa in which all its citizens have an equal chance of prospering. In lieu of reconciliation, what seems to triumph in the final scene of the play is a fundamental and undeniable respect for human creativity. What we are finally left with are two flaming eyes on granite, a reinscription of Nukain Mabuza's story, and with it, the claim: I create, therefore I am.

Just as Nukain's stone garden remains alive in the photographs taken by JFC Clarke and in the series of artworks he created in homage to it over the years, so too, Nukain's painted rocks live in Fugard's play. Mabuza's legacy exists today in the creative endeavors of others. In the same way, Fugard's legacy will be kept alive in the years that lie ahead, embodied every time an actor gives life to one of his characters, every time a reader performs a play for himself, staging it, no less vividly, in the theater of the mind.

But one of the most important questions that *The Painted Rocks at Revolver Creek* leaves us with is what happens, finally, when a creative artist reaches the end of his or her creativity. What happens, when, as Nukain says: "And now . . . here we are. Me and him . . . but I am empty. I got no more flowers in me. So what must I do?" For the now eighty-six-year-old Fugard, these are not theoretical questions, but ones he asks himself every day. For his Helen Martins, it was to blow out her candles one by one, to welcome the inevitable darkness. For his Nukain Mabuza, it was to simply lie down in his pondok and die.

For Fugard, ever the sufferer of enthusiasm ("Hy ly aan entoesiasme," his friend, the Afrikaans author Jan Rabie, used to say), it is to become Dimetos, the character Fugard created in the early 1970s when he was nearly half the age he is now:

> And because of this, his despair was so great that that night he dreamt his hands without himself. A voice was talking to them: "All you ever wanted to do was possess. All you've ever made were tools and machines to help you do that. It is now time for the skills you scorned. Find something and hold it. Close that powerful hand on a thing. Yours. Hold it! The act of defiance man has made his creed. The mortal human hold! Now give it away. Don't be frightened. Only to your other hand. It will still be yours. That's right. Hold it. Tight. That was a terrible second when they were both empty. One still is. Find something. Quickly! Now comes the hard part . . . so listen carefully. Each must give what it has got to the other, at the same time. You must give and take with the same action. Again . . . and again . . ." *(His hands juggle. He starts to laugh . . . and he laughs and laughs)* And now, because your gaiety is so great, the last skill of all . . . Hold them out, and wait . . . *(Curtain)*

—*PF*
Stellenbosch, South Africa
September, 2018

ENDNOTES

1. Tony Kushner, *Angels in America: A Gay Fantasia on National Themes,* first revised combined edition (New York: Theatre Communications Group, 2013), vii.
2. Athol Fugard, conversation with the author, January 29, 2018.
3. John Maizels, *Raw Creation: Outsider Art and Beyond* (London: Phaidon Press, 1996), 158.
4. See JFC Clarke, *The Home of Nukain Mabuza* (Pretoria: Leopardstone Private Press, 2001); see also JFC Clarke, "The Stone Garden of Nukain Mabusa," *Raw Vision: International Journal of Intuitive and Visionary Art* 10 (1994/1995).
5. JFC Clarke, *The Painted Stone Garden of Nukain Mabuza* (Pretoria: Leopardstone Private Press, 2013), 7.
6. Genl. Maj. Chris van Zyl and Dr. Dirk Hermann, eds., *Treurgrond: 20 Jaar van Plaasaanvalle in Suid-Afrika* (Pretoria: Kraal Uitgewers, 2011). After his National Party came into power with the promise of instituting a programme known as apartheid, Daniel François Malan became prime minister of South Africa from 1948 to 1954. "Eendracht" (Dutch for unity or union) conjures up the official motto of the Republic of South Africa from 1961 to 2000, "Eendrag maak mag," or "Unity is Strength."
7. Clarke, *The Painted Stone Garden,* 14.
8. Clarke, *The Painted Stone Garden,* 16.

Glossary

Afrikaner *(Afrikaans)*	A term historically used to refer to a white Afrikaans-speaking South African
Ag *(Afrikaans)*	An interjection similar to "oh"
Aikona *(Fanakalo)*	An emphatic negation
Amanzi *(Zulu)*	Water
Appelkooskonfyt *(Afrikaans)*	Apricot jam
Baas *(Afrikaans)*	Boss; an apartheid-era word with negative connotations today
Bakkie *(Afrikaans)*	A small pickup truck
Bangbroek *(Afrikaans)*	Someone who is easily frightened and does not stand up for himself; literally, "scaredy-pants"

Boer *(Afrikaans)* — Literally, "farmer"; often used to denote an Afrikaner

Bokkie *(Afrikaans)* — A term of endearment; literally, "Small Buck"

Dassies *(Afrikaans)* — Rock rodents found in semi-desert regions of South Africa

Die Here is my herder . . . *(Afrikaans)* — Psalm 23 in Afrikaans: "The Lord is my shepherd . . ."

Dominee *(Afrikaans)* — Reverend

Dominee Crow *(Afrikaans)* — The pied crow, known for its white collar and chest; so named because its markings make it look like a "reverend"

Dompas *(Afrikaans)* — Passbook, an identity document used to control the movement and economic opportunities of black South Africans during apartheid; literally, "dumb book"

Duim *(Afrikaans)* — Thumb

Ewe *(Xhosa)* — Yes

Fokken *(Afrikaans)* — Fucking

Groente *(Afrikaans)* — Vegetables

Haai *(Derived from Xhosa)* — An expression of surprise or disbelief

Hamba *(Zulu, Xhosa)* — Go away

Ja *(Afrikaans)* — Yes

Kaffer *(Afrikaans, derived from Arabic)* — A pejorative term for black South Africans

Klippie *(Afrikaans)* — A small pebble

Klonkie *(Afrikaans)* — A patronizing apartheid-era term for a black or "colored" (a term used to refer to a

	South African of mixed racial heritage) child
Kommando *(Afrikaans)*	A small fighting force, used here to describe a self-organized farm watch
Koppie *(Afrikaans)*	A small hill in an otherwise flat area
Kraal *(Afrikaans)*	A cattle enclosure
Kwas *(Afrikaans)*	Paintbrush
Mielies *(Afrikaans)*	Corn
Miesies *(Afrikaans)*	Missus; an apartheid-era word with negative connotations today
Moeg *(Afrikaans)*	Tired
Mos *(Afrikaans)*	An interjection used for emphasis; in this context, "after all"
Nee wragtig *(Afrikaans)*	Literally, "no, truly"; an emphatic rejection
Onverwacht *(Dutch)*	Literally, "unexpectedly"; here the name of a farm
Oom *(Afrikaans)*	A term of respect for an older man; literally, "Uncle"
Oubaas *(Afrikaans)*	An elderly "baas"
Ouma *(Afrikaans)*	Grandmother; literally, "Old Mother"
Outa *(Afrikaans)*	A paternalistic means of addressing an elderly black man; literally, "Old Father"
Pasop *(Afrikaans)*	Be careful
Polisie *(Afrikaans)*	Police; here associated with the apartheid regime
Pondok *(Afrikaans)*	Shack

GLOSSARY

Skelm *(Afrikaans)*	Crook
Skollies *(Afrikaans)*	Hooligans
Slim *(Afrikaans)*	Intelligent
Sommer *(Afrikaans)*	In this context, "while you're at it"
Stoep *(Afrikaans)*	Veranda
Suka wena *(Zulu)*	Get lost
Tata *(Xhosa)*	A respectful means of addressing an older man; literally, "Father"
Tekkies *(Afrikaans)*	Sneakers
Voetsek *(Afrikaans)*	Get lost
Vredewater *(Afrikaans)*	Literally "Peace Water"; here the name of a farm
Vuka *(Zulu, Xhosa)*	Wake up
Wena *(Common to the Nguni and Sotho-Tswana language groups)*	You
Yo *(Xhosa)*	An expression of surprise or disbelief
Zol *(Slang)*	A hand-rolled cigarette

ATHOL FUGARD is a renowned playwright, director and occasional actor. He was born in 1932 in Middelburg, in the Karoo desert region of South Africa. He has written close to forty plays, four books and several screenplays. His plays include *Blood Knot*, *Boesman and Lena*, *"Master Harold"...and the boys*, *The Road to Mecca*, *The Train Driver*, *The Blue Iris* and *The Shadow of the Hummingbird*. Many of Fugard's works have been turned into films: *Tsotsi*, based on his 1980 novel of the same name, won the 2005 Academy Award for Best Foreign Language Film. Fugard's work spans the period of apartheid in South Africa, through the first democratic elections and Nelson Mandela's presidency, and into present-day, post-apartheid South Africa. One of the most performed playwrights in the world, Fugard is the recipient of many honorary doctorates and awards, the most recent of which was the prestigious Praemium Imperiale global arts prize for Theatre/Film awarded by the Japan Art Association in 2014. At eighty-six, he continues to write from his cottage in the Cape Winelands where he lives with his wife, Paula Fourie, and their dog, Jakkals.

Born in 1985 to a family in the diplomatic service, PAULA FOURIE spent the majority of her childhood in Europe and America, returning to South Africa without having witnessed first-hand the turbulent final years of apartheid. She went on to receive her BMus and MMus degrees from the University of Pretoria, the latter while working as a conductor and teacher at the Drakensberg Boys Choir. In 2013, she obtained her PhD from Stellenbosch University. Paula's published work includes book reviews, interviews, academic journal articles and poetry. She is currently a research fellow at Africa Open: Institute for Music, Research and Innovation at Stellenbosch University. Paula has worked with Athol Fugard in professional theater since 2012, increasingly supporting him in his directorial responsibilities. In 2015, Fugard's *The Shadow of the Hummingbird*—the opening scene of which was written by Paula with the use of Fugard's unpublished notebooks—won a Naledi Theatre Award for Best New South African Script. Paula is currently writing a book based on her doctoral research—a biography of the South African composer and musician Taliep Petersen.